When in doubt, write it out

When in doubt, write it out

BOOK OF POEMS

MARK P. MURPHY

Published by Spines
ISBN: 979-8-89383-328-7

Contents

Introduction

I want to explain that the poems are not all from the same time; most were written during the time of my father's passing. This doctor got me to write poems in my spare time to relieve my pressure from my dad's soon-to-be passing. So, some poems are about my family. And some are just feelings I had growing up as a child. Others were feelings of spiritual adulthood from all the learnings I learned about my faith. The nature of Green Street is about a group home I stayed at while I was out of Riverview. And Riverview is a hospital that I stayed at for a very long time while the hospital and the prison were trying to figure out the right kind of meds for me to take that would calm me down from my outbreaks.

Love

Mother Theresa

Mother Theresa
Made love unique, not for one
But for everyone.

Mark P. Murphy - 8/23/21

Getting Help

Incarcerated
Talk to my social worker
With help, become man

Mark P. Murphy - 9/9/2021

Special Ingredient

Unicorns with might
Legend has it they can do
Powers with their horn

Mark P. Murphy - 9/9/2021

Princess D

Diana of Wales
Had such a shy demeanor
and gave everything

Mark P. Murphy - 9/9/2021

Divine Mercy

St. Faustina Learn
Divine mercy chaplet pray
From Jesus Christ glory

Mark P. Murphy - 4/28/24

First Communion

Communion Learning:
Eat his body, drink his blood
See the saving one

Mark P. Murphy - 4/28/24

M.H.U.S

Men or mice roll this unit.
Even the lowly of low can be here.
Nuts are what we are called.
Tantalizing fools who aren't abnormal.
All it takes is one bad apple for the few.
Legal issues to debate.

He knows he's a man on the outside.
Even though he was a man on both sides.
Always waiting to be persecuted by slaves.
Love comes in and takes over for the meek.
The exact same love that God talks about.
He will love his neighbor like his self.

Ultimately, love comes on God first and foremost.
Nice you will be to the world.
I never want hate to blossom further.
Try and be kind to one and another.

Save the lives of souls from purgatory.
Chance for a choice to change your way.
Understand life and God is where you'll be.

Mark P. Murphy - 9/9/2021

Jesus Came to Earth

Jesus came to earth
Listen anyone who has ears
Fruit of the spirit

Mark P. Murphy - 4/27/24

Holy Spirit

Holy Spirit lives
Heavenly Father glory
This truth will survive

Mark P. Murphy - 4/27/24

Waiting Patiently

A Black Crow on the
winding side of the road,
waiting patiently, eating its roadkill
that's been hit by a slow driving car
in that foggy late night.

The night before it was foggy
and the slow driving car hit a
gray squirrel on the winding
road that he knew so very well.

Instinctively the Black Crow saw
a plump gray squirrel race
back and forth across the road
the black crow knew there would
be roadkill soon.

So, the scavenger, as they are known,
would have a meal that day
on the road killed by a car that
hit the gray squirrel in the foggy
dark night.

Mark P. Murphy - 8/18/21

On Earth

They say heaven is the place
On earth. When you get mace
In your face you know its hell
That you're in. And you're stuck in a cell
And get used to the beat of the white noise
To sleep. Then you wake up turquoise
On your mind. You do the time to pay the price.

Learn from your mistakes
That give you wisdom from the outside.
You stay away from that Jekyll and Hyde
Life. But hold no grudges towards
Friends. Then your back to being on board
Of a lifestyle of a man with time.

Mark P. Murphy - 9/12/2021

On the day he stopped drinking,
New and improved man that he was
Every day was planned for an AA meeting.
Long gone was his habitual old life.
Early on in sobriety he struggled.
Gone was the desire to drink,
Gone was the right leg from alcohol.

Enjoying life with only one leg,
Day after day he led a happy life.
Money to spend on for his children.
Against all odds he had a lengthy sobriety.
Newcomers came and intently listened to him speak.

Mark P. Murphy - 8/11/21

Power Trip

Power trip. Power trip.
That's the most loved position
a person can have in life.
Especially if the person was given a hard time all
through his
growing up being bullied. Or the bully person
stays a bully person to show the power
of others who have no control and
are helpless. Once the bully sees that
he's God, he takes advantage of every
possible action that can be done
to make you show that words speak
louder than actions of fighting.

Mark P. Murphy - 8|24/01

There I see a feather on the ground.
J. Giels says "nighttime is the right time"
I pick up that feather, been released from bound
That I say "daytime is the playtime"
Now then I see playtime is wrong indeed
I read *33 Days to Merciful Love* to understand
But if I'm a Viking there'll be mead
I usually have thoughts that become unplanned
The word "I am" is a very powerful word
This I know from my own firsthand
With all my love I try to bore
A hole in the walls of my room that's bored
All I can do is wait till God tells me my time's up

Mark P. Murphy

Dad's Wisdom

Look on the pavement
See my dad point in the sky
Learn from his wisdom
Reality or memory
Is it fantasy?
Is it real to self!
Find out on other side

Mark P. Murphy - 9/9/2021

Heartbeat

Hearing the beating of your heart
Each day is different, some loud, some faint
At last your heart pulsates the beautiful sight
Rhythmic beating the longer she stays by my side
To me, I know who it is
Better and stronger overjoyed with love
Epiphany I feel for my soulmate showed up
A s tears come from her from seeing me in my state
Teardrops of that beating heart subside as she's gone

Mark P. Murphy 9/10/2021

I was just a lad.

Playing football.

One on one.

He was as big as Goliath on that field.

Every day after school, we'd gear up for our Superbowl.

Finally, in that back-yard stadium.

I could see that endzone.

The uprights behind Sasquatch in Foxborough.

After all failed attempts to get into that endzone,

I talked to a man with wisdom, my Dad.

And then came to play the bowl of players.

With the mindset to play like the 'Tyler Rose',

I made it to the endzone and stood tall,

like the abominable snowmen with stars coming out,

over the competitor who was outplayed by a player who
used his wisdom from Dad

to persevere and became another step towards being a
man.

-Mark P. Murphy   9/6/2021

Family Life

You have many ways in
which you die while living young.
Aborted by family, living sin.
Regret the feeling from what you've done.

Adolescent life is not so fun
when you dream lives of wise guys.
Then you've got a handgun.
You take an oath to swear by.

Unbeknownst to you there's a job
for you to do for your debut,
that involves a gang war in the mob.
Broke your cherry part of a crew.

Eventually living the mob life
you will explore a minute in prison.
Then you miss the good wife,
while you're in prison eating filet mignon
23

By Mark P. Murphy

Girl

That girl a beauty,
a reflection of loveliness.
That girl has spunk,
not full of junk.
That girl won't quit
something she started.
That girl is a mark of loveliness,
her eyes blue as the panthers.
That girl appeals to me,
like ants to sugar.
That girl will be my blueberry
and protect it with strength.
That girl will be my Valentine,
'til the end of time.

By Mark P. Murphy

25

For Better or Worse

Forever I said when I married you
Only family came to our wedding
Really what a beautiful shotgun wedding we had.

Because I meant it when I said for better or worse
Each day is full of sickness, compassionate sickness
Tears come and tears go for yet you're so far but so close
The beating of my heart grows strong on seeing you
Each day I slowly decline. No water, no food.
Race to the end of life.

Of course, I want to be seen by the Blessed Virgin
Rather to ask to intervene for all my sins.

Worked hard for a living

Original man that I was I did for the family
Resulted one love gone to heaven
Sickness ends my life at a slow pace
Every day I look for my soulmate.
27

Mark P. Murphy - 9/10/2021

Both Seeds of Hate

What a life to have in this world.
When your side of hate comes
out of you. Then in an instant a girl
appears. She with all her makeup combs
her hair. To look stylish as usual.

The hate goes away from the mouth
But still builds up on the inside
There still you hear it from the horse's mouth
That you take a left turn Clyde.

Then reaction comes word is stronger
than actions. Then you realize and wonder
just what you're up against in life
and you want to do the strife.

But know there's a time when to do
That. And a time not to. Blood is blue
On the inside. Then turns red which makes
Me go red and not understand.
29

Mark P. Murphy - 9/11/2021

Life

Walking in the colorful, leafy, fall day
I haven't been touched for a lifetime
And a lifetime to God means one day
as thousand years. One minute a day.

Battle this disease. Where I can
Never differentiate between reality
And fantasy. The woods a great way
to get rid of high cost hospital.
Car congestion in traffic.
Able to deal much easier in the country.

While in the woods I came across a unicorn.
Pale, white body, beautiful white
mane and pointed horn that was long,
straight and spiraling sharp.

Now the virgin knew
if she touched that horn her sickness would
leave her and she would be able to carry on with
a beautiful life. So, taking a big chance
I went up to the unicorn to touch
the horn. As I went up to the horn, I felt
transfixed and enthralled and my sickness
left.

Now as I prayed in front of the
unicorn, while on my knees, I could feel air from
all directions. Then as I looked, the unicorn turned
into a Pegasus from granting a wish.

Mark P. Murphy - 9/9/2021

Purgatory

The almighty Lord in al seriousness does not need us,
though we by all means need him if we want
life after death with the evils within us.
Truly we are sinners when we first
wake up, from anytime of the day
to this glorious world called Earth.

We light candles in church and at home
to give hope for that day and
pray we may sanctify our souls
and skip through purgatory and go
right to the first stage of heaven
for a life after that dreadful death.

Mark P. Murphy – 8/11/21

Brick Wall

I came to a brick wall full of vitality in my sleep. Can I go over, under, or around I'll just walk through. It's just a fantasy.

Doors

It only gets better from here when you have many doors to choose from for your journey into a passionate life

-Mark P. Murphy

In Old Age

Theirs prayers to the crucifix
That get answered in Gods time.
The belief of the scars of cicatrix
Scars of such nature are unbelievable....
That any immortal would be eighty-six
To give Jesus that vinegar and gall
So, he can have that quick fix.

Then came back to life from his transfix.
Now you have belief in your prayers.
As you go with the crowd to intermix
Then comes the one Pharoah.
And all the fake politics
Jesus gave each disciple a way.

A priest carries with him pyx.

So, he can give the Eucharist.

Home bound can get their superfix.

Mark P. Murphy – 02/01/24

Confession of Learning

In his time a priest is preaching

Try to give away all teaching.

When I met first priest heart searching

Give confession to show I'm churchgoing!

In front of confessional while toing and froing

Explain all... of your venial sins' wrongdoing!

The priest cares less of all evildoing...

Say the ACT OF CONTRITION like a landing!

Pray 3 Hail Mary's and 1 Our Father satisfying!

Mark P. Murphy - 3/31/24

Great is the staff we work besides...

Residents live in this house abide by the rules...

Even if it means staff gives residents a guide...

Even if a mistake to happen taken by miniscule...

Never weary we have the best of social worker...

Seth works hard to give everyone a refresher...

Theres times laughter made us a tearjerker...

Really all staff pitch in to make it a ground breaker...

Even the residents know the staff has no great worry...

Especially since we know staff can handle any problem...

The other staff that come to help must also take the glory...

Mark P. Murphy - 4/14/2024

Laddie

Gentle is the man that is sentimental....

Especially when found himself a good mentor...

Never was it known that he judgemental...

Thoughtful of the man who is always dead- center...

Love struck is the person who turns sixteen...

Exhausted was the person who had a ponzi-scheme.

Many people are always getting their vaccine...

At time growing up i had the pyramid-scheme.

Never was it known you win being mischievious...

Mark P. Murphy - 4/24/2024

The Winning Aspect

I king Kong to that mighty mouse
That driveway court played every season.
Of our days neighbor cousin in that house.
Blood thicker than water joined by tenons.

I might not have shown it I loved him as a brother.
He showed me how to love even the Bambino.
I love the red sox he Yankees we wait on commentators.
His father the pollack he always went to the casino.

Dazzling as it may all seem we all lived middle class…
When we won it might have been all glamourous
But it really wasn't that so-called victorious…
We went to Chinese restaurants that is very gorgeous.

Mark P. Murphy - 4/24/24

41

The Sounds of Faith

Unmerciful search
By living baptized life lord
One should do this now

Mark P. Murphy - 4/26/2024

Teeth

Thank you, lord for life
I floss, brush, gargle daily
So, to die with teeth

Mark P. Murphy - 4/26/2024

Praying prayers

Exhilerating
Is life with the lord indeed
Never let you down

Mark P. Murphy - 4/26/2024

Lord of all

Magnificent one
Is almighty Jesus Christ
The body is host

Mark P. Murphy - 4/26/2024

The Dreams of my Life

The dream started out of nowhere .... I can't recall the
place when I was in prison.
And the inmates hated me cause I either brought peace
or was screwing all the
Females. And thinking to myself I got to kill someone to
leave. So, I was preparing.
For that day. Then one day in jail a bunch of inmates
trapped me in the sally port.
I looked at it as a sacrifice, but it really was a sacrifice for
another inmate. The
Inmates started pushing in towards the corner of the
four walls squeezing the air...
out of me. Then I started reaching around with my arm
looking for someone's throat.

I found a throat then he looked down I let go because I
thought he wasn't willing to die.
Went over to another throat massaged it with his tattoo
throat and grabbed on tight...
And pulled it and all the inmates smiled. Then I arrived
by waking...

Mark P- Murphy - 3/30/24

END FOR NOW